MARRIAGE

by the same author

poetry
A VIOLENT COUNTRY
AFTER DARK
DREAMS OF THE DEAD
MISTER PUNCH
SELECTED POEMS 1969–1989
NEWS FROM THE FRONT
THE POTTED PRIEST (limited edition)
A BIRD'S IDEA OF FLIGHT

SPRINTING FROM THE GRAVEYARD
(English versions of poems by Goran Simić)
SAVREMENA BRITANSKA POEZIJA
(for the Sarajevo Writer's Union, as editor with Mario Suško)

music theatre
GAWAIN (libretto; music by Harrison Birtwistle)

fiction
FROM AN INLAND SEA

DAVID HARSENT

Marriage

faber and faber

First published in 2002
by Faber and Faber Limited
3 Queen Square London WC1N 3AU
Published in the United States by Faber and Faber Inc.,
an affiliate of Farrar, Straus and Giroux LLC, New York

Photoset by Wilmaset Ltd, Wirral
Printed in Italy

The right of David Harsent to be identified as author
of this work has been asserted in accordance with
Section 77 of the Copyright, Designs and Patents Act 1988

A CIP record for this book
is available from the British Library

ISBN 0-571-21251-4

2 4 6 8 10 9 7 5 3 1

To Julia

Contents

LEPUS

Acknowledgements

Thanks to the editors of the following publications and organisations who first published some of these poems: The Cheltenham Festival, *Independent on Sunday*, *Last Words* (Picador), *London Review of Books*, *The Printer's Devil*, The Salisbury Festival, *Stand*, *Thumbscrew*, *Times Literary Supplement*.

Poem XXIII of *Marriage* makes use of a phrase from an essay on Bonnard by John Berger.

The titles of the poems in *Lepus* are taken from certain section headings (sometimes adapted) in John Layard's *The Lady of the Hare*, a book to which I am indebted in other ways.

Note

Marriage is (very) loosely based on the relationship between Pierre Bonnard and Marthe de Méligny. One rumour has it that their first encounter occurred when he escorted her across the street from Giacometti's studio, another that he saw her getting off a tram, followed her to the place where she worked sewing pearls onto funeral wreaths and simply talked her into going away with him. In any event, she was certainly Bonnard's model thereafter, and for the rest of her life.

After more than thirty years of living together, Bonnard and Marthe decided to marry and Marthe was obliged to reveal that she had lied about who she was. Her name was not Marthe de Méligny but Maria Boursin. Bonnard's reaction is not known. They married and continued to live together until her death in 1942.

D.H.

MARRIAGE

The same pots, carafes, chairs, vases, the same blue
cigarette box, the same oval wicker basket, the same
interiors, the same woman ...

SARAH WHITFIELD, 'Fragments of an Identical World': essay from
the catalogue to the Tate Gallery Bonnard exhibition 1998

I

But arrive like this: a sudden
shadow on the washed-out fleurs-de-lis
that paper the breakfast room; a form half-hidden

by some other form, the angle
of a door, perhaps, unless I think to make it
a shutter, half-open, by which I leave you a single

arm, single eye, single breast, a single link of the scallop-
and-anchor motif on your sun-top, except that I can't
    quite get it
at this point, from just this viewpoint; or else crop up

as someone walking away from the terrace
in a freakish downpour, when reflections
bring the trees indoors and start you again from your
    place

beside the shutter, setting off bravely from a house of
    rain,
not even half-visible, now, then barely
visible at all, then gone.

II

In the more or less conventional Nude
Descending a Staircase, there's this rub of verticals,
flesh and wood,

enough to make any man's fingertips prickle.
A sudden stumble would make things that bit more
    tactile,
but a foot going out from under,

a slip-and-stagger,
a wild, almost-airborne grab at the stair-rail,
ends up in this openly crude

legs-akimbo sprawl, a crooked pink smile
as you hawk in your breath and hang on fast to your
    footsoles,
head dropped, like someone woken by cramp

flexing the tendon, everything down to a hum and out
    of focus,
as if that first free breezy descent, toes afloat,
was a dream all the while.

But even after you've left, you've left this lip of damp
in the shape of an aspen leaf where you plumped
down on the chequerboard tile

that runs out from the hall
to the kitchen. Close back here, I watch you bring
a pan to the hob,

one knee tucked, one shoulder a touch off true,
as you wait for the water to sing ... at which you step
down from the door to a cold silver slub

of dew and cross the terrace, the ankle-deep lawn, the
    almost-blue
of our geranium wall, searching, I guess,
for mint for mint tea. Still naked. And still at risk

what with the god of the kitchen range to burn you, the
    god
of the garden end to twist
his bramble about the thin white spindle of your waist.

III

We are naked: as it might be, after sex; but there's a
    screen
cutting you off from me, or me from you. I stand
much closer to the world, although you seem

to take most of the light, and lean
back on the bed, one leg tucked up, one hand
reaching to pet the cat. 'The world at large' is what
    I mean.

On your side a trace of musk or ambergris, on mine
whisky and the sting of turpentine,
as if we had marked our ground, as if we had staked a
    claim,

you to play the odalisque, me to set a stain
on your linen, then up and turn my back and work till
    dawn.
You tell me your dreams are bad; I say the same.

It's as if we could still be here in thirty years
with more possessions but fewer needs, your name
on the very tip of my tongue, and mine on yours.

A hunter's moon hangs in the bathroom steam.
Tell me where you learned that a daily soak
in that scald was more than halfway to a cure

for whatever might ail you – some compendium
on Health and Welfare for the Modern Woman?
Was it a footnote in that same vade mecum

that encouraged you to seek
comfort in darkness, so you rise from the bath and draw
the shadows to your shoulders like a cloak?

Come back to bed: there's more
to be done to this double portrait, double take.
Man and Wife, Nude; or man and wife in the raw.

IV

Here's your great rival and mine: by Degas, perhaps, or
    Lautrec.
How would she look on ice: how would she look
with a hole in her heart or a spike in her eye or a rope
    round her neck?

V

Have you put a touch of auburn to your hair? That's
    new.
It helps. So does the dab of blusher and lip-
gloss: 'Carmensita'; now, if I look hard, it's you

and not you, playing slip-
the-noose in a swarm of dapple by our geranium wall.
How is it you know me so well if I scarcely know you at
    all?

'Slip-the-noose', with its little ball and chain . . .
Or you tackle your second whodunnit
of the day, your second Margarita, alone,

or not alone if that's the way you want it –
I could touch in a rose, 'Sang de Boeuf', amid the green,
nothing simpler, or drop a linnet

on the one true blackened bough on the one dead tree
in all the orchard, then join you for this plain
lobster, lemon wedge, tomato salad, cherries, brie,

your Margarita set aside
for a crisp rosé, as the wholly unmatchable calf's-eye
blue begins to flood with crimson lake, a bad

blackwater backwash pouring through like smoke.
You crack a claw. We take up pliers and probes. The
    garden
develops into darkness stroke by stroke.

When I get back with candles – camphor and
    sandalwood –
there's just the sound of your bath filling up, and a
    sudden
mush of radio music. Your hair is up in a snood

to keep it dry while you read
those last few pages. The slither of pink in the S-bend
is the final clue to 'The Mystery of the Red Hand'.

VI

This is you and me making love in the all-but dark.
Here's a glimmer of light from an eye, a glisten of spit
    on an eye-tooth.
We are playing Hide My Face and Ape the Turk.

Later, I turn up the lamp and shadows flock
to the corners of the room, except those that huddle
along the dint of your spine, or pool in the small of your
    back.

The lamplight falls bang in the middle
of the almost-oval mirror on your grandmamma's
    armoire,
its unearthly sprays of violets, its darker growth

of badpenny foxing. See how we stare . . .
Which brings me face to face with the stony riddle
of who you want to be, or who you are.

Morning catches us both in a different light,
one shaping up to the day, the other gone deep beneath
the dump of the coverlet, a twist of hair, a pair of
    wholly innocent feet.

VII

Wouldn't it just about cover that damp by the lintel,
this foggy junk-shop oil
of Mary and Martha done as a mirror-image? It's easy
  to tell

who's who, what with her foxy hair, the blip of a nipple
under rose satin, a smile blurred by kissing;
easy enough, what with the cruel pull

of her plait, the keys on her belt, the gruel-ladle.
Already I'm harried by thoughts of what might be
  missing
beneath that undyed dimity; already I'm itching to
  stipple

that satin with spittle, and so I would
if I could talk her down from lintel to mantel,
from mantel to hearth, and live with her, side by side,

while her dumpy double
guards the threshold, though things might so easily go
  to the bad,
that first loose look, that soon-to-be-final betrayal.

VIII

You remember that movie, don't you? – the rain like
    grapeshot
on a drum, the banged-up Pontiac
pulling over at the pump, a sideslip of red hot

jazz from the radio, the screen door creaking and
    slapping
as she makes an appearance, wiping her hands
on her apron, a link of impossibly bright hair slipping

free of its French pleat. 'Got some coffee?'
'Coffee? Yeah.' 'Got somethin' to eat?' You can see the
    strands
of their lives pulling into a knot as soon as they get
    squiffy

and put that slow-slow song with the aching sax
on the nickelodeon, while she gives her life to date:
'Ma 'n' pa 'n' him.' It's clear as day there's a big black
    hex

on this random throw of the bones, this coming
    together;
it's there in the music, there in the grey-green weather.
Coming together too soon if not too late.

He earns his bacon and beans with a coat or two of
    paint
on the barn, or by cutting and stacking live oak for the
    stove.
Remember the freckle of sweat along the faint

line of down on her lip when she sits on the porch
to watch him split the first cord? Remember his poor
white cardsharper's back; the way his reach

doesn't match up to his swing? Remember the muddle
    of mauve
shadows across the kitchen blind . . . ? Him with one eye
    on the door,
her in the peach peignoir, asking what he'd give.

'Do you love me?' she wants to know, and he says, 'Sure.'
'Do you?' 'Sure.' 'Do you *love* me?' 'Sure I do.'
And all that follows this proceeds from fear,

not least the day-for-night in that dusty store room,
feed bags and nose bags, the crucial claw-
hammer, the equally crucial yardbroom,

where she lets him wrangle her onto the tar-paper floor,
down like a dog, unblinking, her five and dime
crucifix ticking against her chin each time

his face comes into shot. Remember that?
Did she ever tell him her name?
Wasn't his, in any case, a *nom de guerre*?

You sat, if I've got it right, still wearing your hat and coat
against the chill . . . Our local café, a small plate of
    crevettes,
a glass of the crisp Sancerre you'd taken to your heart

that summer. Didn't we decide, right away, it was a
    sham? –
the fruity saxophone, a girl who'd fall for such a creature,
greys and greens you never find in nature.

IX

I have you to a T, that oh so
economical crucifix, an apple tree
as it happens, ring-barked just below

the growth point, and hacked
to a stumpy stillness; yes,
have you tooth and nail, that slack

tilt of the head, arms hidden, as if tied
at the wrist or the elbow, eyes all but closed.
Who do you want her to be? The Bondage Bride?

The Girl Who Tamed the Unicorn?
Perhaps she was drawn to the stifled music
in this very tree, much as you and I are sworn

to the edge of things, to the black drop,
never a place to find your future,
never a place to look back,

but even now you turn
to what must be a trick of the light if it's not the tip
of that glittering horn, though this is never

a place to expect such a creature,
come in the hope of apples, its sweet slaver
creaming you as its head falls to your lap.

X

Is this your magic or mine? – One moment
we are in the Street of Songs or the Street
of Locks, fast in the flyblown south, the next in this city
    apartment

among the old stuff you liked to carry from place
to place, the whigmaleerie that seemed no more than a
    sea-
smoothed fist of glass, except you could all but find your
    face,

deep there, a speck in a moonstone, a freckle in an
    otherwise
bright eye, the could-be-accidental jot
on a canvas from which all else must rise

and take shape, bringing us by and by to a roofscape,
to a certain roof, to a certain room, in fact, beneath
the eaves, where you sit frozen-faced, wearing only a
    lacy cape

of north light, the roofscape your backdrop, the jot
    itself nothing more
than a freckle of green set deep
in your wide grey eye. Look at the way the morning cold
    seems to draw

a blue glow to your skin, look at the way your blue lips
    blur,
the way your breasts soften in blue, the way blue
    shadows fall
to your lap. Come to think of it, I'm almost sure

it was on that very morning you finally reached an end
of winter and nakedness and the slow blue stroke
I brought to your cheekbones. 'South. Let's go south.
  We'll send

for whatever we need, whatever we might forget. This
  blue
will be the death of us. Can't you picture it? –
sunlight, a running sea, the house laid open to such
  winds as blow . . .

You could work till you wept, ignoring the eternal
  rights and wrongs
that trouble northern men, myself, meanwhile, let loose
to kick my heels up in the Street of Songs.'

For you a handful of the smuggled calamata, for me a
   good wide bite
of the humble bummalo as I fetch what's needed to set
the table, there, where the last of our crystal gives back
   something to the night.

I have opened the doors to the terrace. Those blacks
   that float
so lethally on blue can only be the shadows of owl and
   stoat
out to kill what they can. Looking at things from here,
   I see how I might

locate you by those very doors so as to put you almost
   out of sight,
head lowered, of course, face turned aside, but just
   enough left to irritate
the eye, what with your scarlet dress, the crewel-work
   aconite

on each point of the collar, what with the hint of
   something indiscreet
in the loft of your shoulder, the unravelling of your
   plait.
Warm bread, now; a dish of salt ... Hear that? – it's
   fight or flight

out there in the borderlands, out there it's murder by
    rote;
but you enter with a tray, standing a moment in that
    self-same spot,
and a dark breeze rearranges your hair so it's nearly but
    not quite.

Each evening in this room, and still I can't get you right:
that sideways glance I'm after comes half a glance too
    late,
then your hands go wrong, and your mouth, as you dip
    your head to eat:

for you the calamari and calabrese, for me a sweet
cut from a well-hung hare. Will you try a taste from my
    plate?
This morsel, perhaps, with its fats and juices intact.
    Take it. My treat.

XII

Going in after you, I'm treated to the sour, nutty odour
of your first-things-first deliverance of ordure,
something like geraniums gone over.

Sitting where you sat, I picture
the loops, the pinkish links, the suety tucks of viscera,
jejunum, cæcum, ileum, the backed-up bacteria,

the pale plantations of flora,
just as I do those nights beneath the sheet when I go in
    after
you, face first, then sometime later

rest my head on your hip and catch the low-down
    laughter
deep in your gut, a burbling from ponds and swamps
    and backwater
swims that brings with it a whiff of sulphur

such as I'm getting now, which I know will grow sweeter
in the telling than sherbert or attar
of roses or the rich mahogany cloud from your hothouse
    exotica.

XIII

See the lake at sundown, crimson lake, crimson
sky, save one broad bolt of blue laid on a blue
so deep you might not catch the tension

between the two and see it black.
Now see yourself asleep, just where I left you:
in that boat out on the lake,

hitched to a painter hitched
to a pier securely pegged to terra firma,
your face perfect to catch

the glow that draws the sky down to the water;
but see how the loop on the bowline
slips as the boat beam-ends

waves put up by the wind. The faster
they come the more the bow leans
to the offshore drift, its slant

drawing a long firm line to the sharp-
angled funnel-and-sluice of the vanishing-point
where the lake gives on to the sea and the sea

to more of the same if you keep
that bearing; and finally open your eyes
to the Chinese-white of the sky, fierce, with another
    white

washed on, that could be the wings
of petrel and kittiwake,
while beneath you the ultramarine now flows

into darker shades of blue, of blue and blue-black,
something better suited to pen and ink,
and yourself in that edgeless waste, not knowing who
    to thank.

XIV

'The artist's wife with flowers', if not, 'With cat
couchant' is how I conjure some such pet
filling your lap; or geraniums, freshly cut.

This face and that face, turn and turn about.
The cat filching a bloodbead; petals pink and wet
opening to the touch. What you see is what you get.

Now rise from the bath, your hair caught up with a peg.
The water peels back from your breasts like the film
    from a cooking egg.
You cleanly cleave your arse as you lift one leg

to the edge of the tub and start to work the towel
from ankle to thigh, then into the damson bevel
of your crotch, after which you sit, heel to knee,

on a raffia chair, your quim guerning to a scowl
as you slip your foot into the foot
of your stocking. Next, it's your face coming free

of the summer dress, as you greet
yourself in the mirror. Here's how it goes after that:
    foundation, powder, eye-
shadow, blusher, mascara,

lipstick pressed to a tissue ... that perfectly mute
syllable of love (love, or it could be hate)
that I pick up and pocket to re-read later.

The same summer dress you loosened and dropped with
    a clatter
of tiny buttons on tile as I backed you up to the table,
our first night under this roof, and you The Biddable

Spouse, slipping your foot out of the foot
of your stocking ... The same table
you cover with a red checkered cloth, setting the bread,
    the butter,

the plum preserve, and the best we have of china.
Ur-wife. Wife of wives.
I'm close enough for ambush as you pass with your box
of knives.

XVI

I perch on a 'Bauhaus-style' chrome and raffia
stool as you drop your knife and pause to consider
this fish and its fistula,

this fish with its deep deformity, its head like a cosh,
its raw flank and blood-brown eyes,
its lips of lopsided blubber,

this fish we are having for supper.
You laid out cold cash
to have them deliver this fish, close-packed in ice,

a glacier coelacanth preserved against all the odds,
as if some throw of the dice, some coin
turning a thousand years to come down heads,

had brought to the marble slab in our kitchen
of all kitchens this fish, sporting
its jowly truncheon-lump of sorbo rubber

and the great wet ulcer opening beneath its backbone.
As you start again, flensing good from bad, you let spill
a viscous flub of gut that slips

from your wrist to the marble, where it spells
out the hierogram most often linked
with the once in a lifetime, miraculous

descent of the goddess, her gills
crisp enough to cut as you trade kiss for kiss.
Flesh of her flesh. I'll eat it if you will.

XVII

In your dream we are separated by war
and after untold business somehow make our way
to the café where they keep that bright Sancerre.

It has taken half a lifetime. You in a window seat
writing a letter, me at the window unable to make out
who it's for. You smile and sip your wine: Pouilly Fumé.

I have fifty blacks to hand which are really black
with a bit of this, if you look, and a bit of that.
I am saving the darkest dark for such a day.

XVIII

A still life is how I see it – a cool approach
to a book, a bowl of stones, a peach,

and, as luck would have it, our neighbour's gift of a hare,
its brittle foot, its bloodsoaked eye, fur

that flows to the touch –
so what should I think when you turn up, standing a bit
   too far

or not quite far enough: there and not there
like rain in the sun, like a spoke in a turning wheel?

Look, if I bring you into this, as I sometimes have before,
what's the most I can get – a shoulder and heel

as you slope off into the hall?
A broken smile, perhaps, your passe-partout?

When you open the door you alter the light: not much,
but enough to put those objects out of reach . . .

And what will it be goes with you when you go?
Next to nothing, it seems. A small bite from the peach.

XIX

Who do you want to be? I think I ought to know.
If someone stood beyond me to watch this portrait grow,
backing off to size you up, then me, he might decide

there's really nothing to choose, and less to hide;
I could become you at a stroke
and open up to darkness. We stand here, toe to toe,

as I add what's yours to you: these votives and charms,
a junkyard of feather and glass and stone, any one of
    which
possesses the power to put you beyond harm,

as we know, bringing them, touch by touch, to a low
Chinese lacquered table just beyond your reach.
Everything here is exactly what it seems:

the down on your lip, the tuck of your dress, the slow
blade of the ceiling-fan, the window reflecting all this;
    and beyond
the window, a balcony; and beyond, a city street,

and beyond even that, an alley, a rat-run sloping to
    shadow,
the *via negativa* where nothing can come to good.
What if you and I were to meet

a year from now by that self-same alley, mad
for each other, just as we were, just as we ought to be,
    and go
hand in hand to the end, and then beyond?

Would you still have this picture of us in your head?
Would it turn out to be the last thing we ever did?
Would you be glad?

XX

Not the turn of a card, not the casual spin of a knife,
not some image in a glass, not the guidance of glass, not
   glass
rolled to a gleam by the surf, not yourself, the spaewife,

up to your wrists and beyond in the hot
purples and pinks of the hen's most secret inner life,
can tell what this weather portends: a coarse

wind, a tinfoil sun, the sky coming closer to land
with each pull of the sea. The window is open and there
   you sit, your face
bruited against the light, exactly right, except I have to
   use

dark charcoal against the sudden grey. It will last all
   week
if it doesn't clear by noon; do you think you could stand
to go out in it later, to walk by the water, to keep

still long enough, at least, to be caught half-hidden,
   half-lost
in a cross-hatch of rain; and white coming off the waves
   as if to test
the stripe of white on your cheekbone, the white on
   white of your fist

as you clutch your collar and look down the line of the
   bay
where the sea piles in, rack after rack after rack?
Could you? It doesn't matter if not: we'll spend the rest
   of the day

on the blind side of things, and stay,
me with my drink and book, you with your back
to the window, the beat of the sea, the deepening
  aftershock.

– here, cutting bread. Your knife, at that high angle,
reminds me of Holofernes, of Sisera, but later makes me
    think
of *The Death Wish in Women*: that useful hank

of hair Kokoschka gives his man to hold, to yank
the head right back, to draw the throat like a bow, and a
    single
swipe with the knife will do the trick. And here again, at
    the sink

to hulk a chicken, up past your wrists in the red-blue
    tangle
to nip out the liver and heart, to draw the heartstring.
Remember our first day together? – your new-fangled

hat, my sober suit and cravat, that bold Sancerre, the
    headstrong
pledges that leave me now with nothing to do but watch
as you stoop to that very same sink to loosen your hair,
    to let it dangle

under the flow; nothing to do but try to catch
the way you soap and rinse and twist it dry, then
    suddenly arch
your neck to throw it back, a model for so-and-so, or
    such-and-such.

XXII

There are three of us then, you full-face to the mirror
and me directly behind you on the bed
looking out from behind the spread of the morning
    paper
as you fetch out, piece by piece, your impedimenta.

You can see I'm not doing what I should:
not working my way through the front-page drama
of 'the gathering storm'; instead
I'm watching a storm as it gathers,
piece by piece, across the stretch of water
that flows between our scrap of beach and the harbour.

The bay is black, and the cape, and the heavy red-blue-
    red
on the skyline is putting out livid tracers
the way an infection will start off small but spread,
reaching out to the heart.
                                        You snap shut the lid
of your compact. What next? Eye-shadow, eyeliner,
    mascara,
the dark-eyed, morbid look of the virgin martyr.

Yes, I can work with this: your face, the back of your
    head,
your naked back, my face over your shoulder,
see how it all adds up? And then the weather . . .

As for what lies beneath, take it as read.

XXIII

This landscape was first called 'Landscape', then 'A Walk
in the Country', then 'The Uphill Path'.
Your hand in mine; and there, in the palm, an unmissable
    fork

in the heartline. Even so we set out
on a day of broad skies, I seem to remember, and stark-
white cumulus rolling through. The map rumpling
    under our feet.

~

Just as I seem to remember starting
in the usual way with the canvas tacked to the wall, the
    window
open to a day of broad skies, and loading the brush, and
    thinking

that anything – a love affair, a marriage – could start
in the self-same way, even a simple walk
in the country; one step, one leap of the heart.

~

'This could be as good a place as any
to kiss you off, to watch you slowly shorten
as the hill rises, to make this the last of many

fond farewells.' I smiled at that. We had gone about a
    mile
and stopped to listen to birdsong, not that we could tell
linnet from wren, or thrush from nightingale.

~

Though anyone would know it was a thrush that lay
on the path, broken open, dust in its eye,
wings spread wide as if to block our way,

a gift to divination ... But once you'd knocked away
the crust of blow-fly grubs and got right down to the
    decay
there was nothing to tell; or else you wouldn't say.

~

Much later, you would insist
it was a day like any other '...wind rushing the poplars,
brief rain, sunlight on distant water...' and the rest.

But you turned and hiked your skirt up and half sat
to let go a stream of piss that cut the dust,
a delicate yellow delta. You must have forgotten that.

~

Such brief rain as drove us into the lee
of a hilltop obelisk, with a view clear down to the sea
and a much closer view of some lilac-and lime graffiti

sprayed on the stone.   *THAT BINT*
GOES APE THE TURK   LA DAME DE LA BELLE ÉPOQUE
   – HER JUICY CUNT
ODI PROFANUM VULGUS   BOOT BOYS   UBI SUNT

~

Coming down from there, you gave me a blow-by-blow
account of where they were,
those bits and pieces of mine that had all gone into the
    blue,

or so I thought. Something swerved hard and ran off
on the blind side of a hedge.
'You kept them, then, even though ...' 'Yes, all safe, all
    safe.'

~

No question in my mind that this was the Angel of
    Death,
amanita virosa, its blunt white head, white gills,
tell-tale 'flaring annulus', the fleshy white sheath

at the base with its payload of filth,
while you were pretty sure it was *amanita*
vaginata, safe to pluck up and take home and eat in
    good health.

~

The obelisk now at our backs ... Your hair caught up in
    a pleat
just as it was on the day we met
outside that other man's studio, you oddly quick on
    your feet

as we crossed the road in the rain, holding on to our
    hats
and dwindling, from his point of view, in the dwindling
    light.
'The more I take away, the bigger it gets.'

~

When we came to that low bridge, you led, I followed,
hanging back to find the moment
when light fell on the water and you were swallowed

by brightness, your form a dark flare
at the heart of things ... you were there
and not there, as always; lost in the near.

~

Over here, the smell of wild garlic, the roll of the sea;
over there, a way into the wood
and the world growing silent under the canopy.

As for what happens next, if someone's to blame
it might as well be me.
As for which way to go, things are just as they seem.

~

'Who in hell would take a spray-can way up there?'
It was all downhill after that,
heading back the way we'd come, heading into the glare

of the setting sun like those thin silhouettes at the end
of a Hollywood movie, winnowed by light,
and soon coming down to nothing but straws in the
    wind.

Full-length in the bath, you are wasp-
waisted, long-legged, high-breasted: you are just as you
    were.
The water is skimmed with sunlight from the cusp
of your feet to the wide weed of your hair.

It's best for me if I'm standing on a chair,
back a bit and off to the side: where I always stand,
in fact, to get you right, to watch you pour
those syrups and crystals, to watch the colours blend,
to watch you wallow as if it were kill or cure.

Which could, you want to tell me, be the case.
The sun dips under the sill; a fragile gloss
peels off the bathroom tiles and the water greens.
You slip below the surface with open eyes.

Don't you know that total immersion will soften your
    bones?
Don't you know what it signifies to fold
your arms across your breasts like that? It must be cold
so far down, and dark. Can you hear the drone
of deep-sea psalmody, or feel the tides?

Come up from the salt and I'll give you back the sun
flourish by flourish, just as it was, green into gold.

XXV

I hope to see myself better than ever like this,
the light full in my face, the mirror close enough to kiss.

I could sketch someone in, just lightly, or someone's
    shadow,
at the other end of the room, unless she's at the window

and I'm getting a double reflection, glass to glass,
as she takes the long view

of this same house, same room, same furniture, same face
looking back in puzzlement and love. Is it you?

If it is I want you to know I never knew
how close things sometimes lay between fear and farce

those times in the hard-baked south with an offshore
    blow
pinning us down for days,

me locked away with my gift and the ounce or two of
    grace
needed to work it well; you ... somewhere about the
    place.

So much for your 'demi-Paradise'.
So much for my 'waking dream'.

Just as here in the mirror, things are not what they seem:
someone or other turning away, which leaves

a portrait in monochrome
of a blind man breaking through to a lightless room.

XXVI

The sight of my face, my own face turned around, is all
   I need
to bring me to the edge, the edge
of tears, although if you looked across the bonescarp of
   my head

at the scaly moonscape that fades each morning from
   the glass,
you'd find me dry-eyed, too terrified
to weep for what I've come to. A fine thing. A pretty pass.

Bit by bit I touch myself in,
the grey-green highlights in flesh, the bright bone
winking through the skin,

until I've had more than my fill of colour and line;
and when the whole thing's done
I shall hang my head, my heavy head, on a peg

with a clear view of the garden,
in the hope of finding you going from row to row
between the peas and the calabrese,

or in among the raspberry canes with their rig
of muslin and chicken-wire, you with your broken-
   handled hoe,
you in your bombazine blouse,

you in that old straw hat, grubbing up each fair-weather
   weed,
unless you're already dead
of course, unless that's where this scrutiny of flesh, of
   flesh and bone comes in.

If you could make it back, if you could be here
to see how I see myself these days: the bitter drear,
'Still Life with Bad Fruit and Turnip-top', 'Landscape

with Junkyard and Quarry', if you could make the leap
from wherever you are to wherever I am, you'd see the
    press of fear
in each brushstroke, the sad lack of scope,

the way things are well on the way to that final *Sorry* . . .
And you'd see that I'm doing the best I can to get clear
of all the old stuff we used to carry

back and forth each year from the coast to the city,
you with every manner and make of keep-
sake, from the dead heads of your wedding posy

to a novelty mirror that showed the unguarded rear
of the Rokeby Venus, so plump and pretty
that any man might hope

to leave his mark there somehow, sharp and deep;
the posy, the mirror, a glass rock worn to the shape
of whatever you want it to be, memento mori,

its bare brow raddled and scarred
like the almost-touchable moon that tipped each tree
in turn as we sat, you and I, in our own backyard

some far-off night, half-hearing the rack of the sea
on pebbles and sipping wine and eating a tart tapenade
and never thinking it would be

like this, never thinking things would be quite this hard,
even during those darkest of all dark nights when we lay
in a coddle of sweat, side by side

but also back to back, defenceless, our sleep
spoiled by dreams in which one of us turned a card
and the worst of the future was laid out, plain to see.

If you could just step up, if you could be lured
back from in-between, if that's where it is, I could turn
the lot over to you: the glass whatnot, the seed-

pods from your nosegay, that ludic card, the Rokeby's
    fat backside,
these *late self-portraits where the stern*
gaze, set deep in a fleshless head,

seems for all the world – since you alone might learn
how they find us, these follies, and what they mean,
and whether to lay them up or watch them burn.

LEPUS

The man proposes to the hare that they should kill their mothers

We took it straight from the plot
of 'Strangers on a Train', both of us hot
impavidi et impunes matrem occidere. She grinned
a gappy grin: 'Do you want to or not?'

'Picture it,' said the beast, 'I've sinned
and you've sinned and there we sit
absolved by symmetry. Two on the trot.'
She danced a rickety jig. 'What pranks!'

What could I say but 'Thanks, yes, thanks a lot.'

The hare's skin in the moon's face

Lickety-spit. She can double round
to the dark side, leaving a puff of dust and a tidy mound
of pellets to mark her place.

She'll play you lost and found
in the Sea of Snakes and reappear
as that actress (you'd know the face)
rehearsing 'The Death Wish in Women': her new play.

It's a game of catch
as catch can in which the near and dear
is always slightly risky and far away,
and the creature herself runs rings at such
speed she arrives as she leaves, sauntering up to where
her other self hangs fire in unbreathable air.

The hare man makes the best sexual partner

And the hare woman knows as much: that itch,
that throb in the crotch if she happens to bring him
   to mind . . .

She likes it best when he comes to her in the dark,
hide and seek, it is, where one must find
the other, turn and turn about. Most often, he'll leave
   his mark
on some soft part, the nape
of the neck, perhaps, where he fastened his teeth
to fix her as he made his leap.

Does she love him? Not in the least:
how else could she send him away, or trust
him ever to return – his winning ways, his soft soap –
or choose to come to his call, or spread to his fist?

And what does the hare make of this, watch as she must?

The hare enjoys being hunted

'Have you heard a pack give tongue? There's nothing
    finer –'
she started across the scorch-marks in the stubble
without so much as a glance over her shoulder.
'I run in circles, each one slightly smaller
(you'll notice) than the last: it saves the trouble
of a long, cross-country haul and keeps them eager,
having sight of me now and then. I play the feeble
bag of bones to let them gain some ground,
or leap a valley and skim a rising river,
leaving them so far behind
that I have to tag some gorse or a stand of elder
with piss to keep them in the game; or, better,
show my lily-white scut across an acre
of ploughland, bringing them on until the sound
of the horn and their belling gets louder
than I like to allow: the point where I smell each hound
by name and feel their slaver
freckle my fur ... which means it's time to deliver
myself of the kind of flourish
you'd expect, as I go head first and – *hoopla!* – vanish
up the nip and tuck of my own vagina.'

The man tries to burn the hare but fails

Spiked on a spit, staked out above the fire,
she simply will not roast. I like it *bleu*,
but this much blood ...? She's not just rare, she's raw.

~

La Pucelle, St Catherine, some other martyr on a
    griddle...
With one bound – *ha!* – she steps into the middle
of next week. Solve that riddle.

~

She laughs and leads them on: folklorists and scholars.
In the farthest field, a reaper holds up a brand
braided from the final stand
of corn on the final day. 'Ho! – the hare's neck,' he
    hollers.

~

The goodwife branded a witch and brought to this pyre
    of green
branches still in leaf
is their means to ecstasy, their means to grief.
White-eyed, she stares them down until her pain
ushers in this endless rain.

~

Into the furnace, then; but when I turned
she was standing right there, wearing a trick of the light
which she dropped with a chuckle: *Yes it's me all right.*
So who was it screamed when the door slammed shut?
  Who burned?

The hare as witch animal

'I can use any one of the nine God-given portals
to slip inside the old bitch, catch
her dozing on the settle,
knees at a bawdy angle, her hand still clutching the
    bottle,
then wake her and take her out
to fret their corn with mould and leave their cattle
hamstrung amid the eyebright and the vetch.

While she's stripped and whipped I go to ground,
hunkered beneath her ribs but in fine fettle
(since you ask) and alive to the cries and laughter as
    they fetch
the stool and bring her tethered to the pond
under a sudden rain of stones and spittle.

It's sink or swim for Mother Dark; I've already found
the back way out. Look, there I go at full stretch
between magic and mortal.'

The hare as fecundatrix

The massive chalk excavation best seen from the air
or a vantage-point twenty miles off, is known as The
*   Great White Hare,*
sometimes as Selena, or else The Sixpenny Maid ...

where they come at night with their men, the women
    who prayed
and got no answer, to go belly-up on her dugs
or, if not belly-up, face-down and ridden bare-
back through the night, all the time calling for more,
more, more, wanting to get the last of it, even the dregs.

And moonlight back off the chalk is the light of their eyes
when first they see the mooncalf, and hear its cries.

Cutting the hare

Always remember: knife to leveret
not leveret to knife – the old wives' caveat.
She turned him up, teasing the testes out.

The whole company, then, in single file
to touch him for luck, and wild music and, as a rule,
invocations that play on the word for 'steel
when struck by moonlight'.

Be ready with cap and bells ...
Now she's got him right, now she's set him straight,
the hare bows down before the Holy Fool.

The white hare called 'bright eyes'

Made up to a pout-and-blush, trailing a brand new coat,
her diamante clip, in the shape of a crescent moon,
catching the on/off pink and purple neon,
she makes tracks for Michabo's place downtown
where the barman fixes her usual: a vodkatini, straight
up with a twist, then another, then a third, all of
    them bought
by that stud in the grey fedora and pearl stickpin
who believes he's been here before, believes he's seen
enough to know who's up for what, and who's going flat
on whose back back at whose place later. As he lights her
    cigarette
he gets the full force of her lashless gaze
and a smile, what's more, of such infinite grace
as would bring any man to his knees … and you can bet
he'll find himself in just that position, some time near
    dawn,
in the far reaches of –, a warmish wind in his face,
the last few stars fading back into the haze,
and nothing to say what he's done or where he's been.

The hare as bad omen

They paunched her and got the answer they deserved.

A long dark winter will follow a long dark night
of the soul, everything fading away, everything in retreat,
from little more than black looks and black thoughts
to a black hole squeezing the very last of the light
when the world is halved and the half is halved and
     the half
halved again, and thus, until its density and weight
are greater, even, than those of the human heart;
when oceans resolve to a water-bead, and a ragged scarf
of sky twists about itself like the helix of life
drawn out to an endless thread then gone with a
     snap-and-roar;
when creation, you might as well know, comes down
     to nothing more
than the pinpoint crystal eye of the trilobite.

She got up out of her crimson and ran about, unzipped
like a pyjama-case, laughing her trademark laugh.
'It seems you got more than you hoped.
Better, my darlings, you had set aside my chitterlings
and dished them up with mash and liquor, better
you'd bagged me and jugged me and spread
some Melba toast with a little patum peperium,
or tossed my hams in batter,
or stewed me into silence – yes, better
by far than to know these things which, no matter
your bells and candles, no matter your half-
measures, your few steps back, will come, will come,
     will come.'

The hare as willing sacrifice

My blood and bowels went to the black broth of Sparta.
The milk from my dugs washed the face of the whore
   Luxuria.
My flesh was a gift outright to the kings of Tara.

My pelt is a chaperon, will you wear it?
My head is a fount of wisdom, will you share it?
My scream is the last of me, can you bear it?

Fire the transforming medium

The sulphurous gleam in her eye is the light of a match
struck half a mile away
and cupped and laid to the tip of a torch.

Time enough, surely, to make a getaway ...
But no, she'd sooner lie up, the better to catch
(floating between the sheaves) that rich
smell of scorch; the better to watch
as the circle closes, to hear their voices, to play
'duck-and-dive' or 'doggo' or 'dead in a ditch'.

In the last field, now, they kindle the last of the corn.
There she goes, wearing her crown of fire as to the
    manner born.

The hare as a symbol of the repentant sinner

Flat on her face in the dust.
Flat on her face in the dust with your boot on her neck.
Flat on her face in the dust with your boot
on her neck, she confessed
the worst of it (which, at the time, she probably thought
    the best).

You listened, although it made you sick.
You listened, although it would surely bring you awake
at three a.m. that night and every night,
hard-pushed by a dream where she spilled into the dust
the same Christ-awful mess
which you'd stir with the toe of your boot
like roadkill, like something slaughtered in flight.

And do you truly repent? *I do.*
And do you offer atonement for sin? *I do.*

(She's kneeling, now, and tugging your sleeve.)

For all I let slip
I hereby give you leave
to notch my ears in kind, to slit my nose and lip.

The hare as love charm

Jugged-up she is all dark meat,
weeping from brow to heel. Her eyes are white,

as you can see; a web of veins in the pelt
still runs blue-black. Discard all that. Now draw aside

the blood and mix with wine. Bring up the heat
to sear the flesh. Watch how the nuggets of fat

render down. Good. Leave her to stew
in her own juice for half a day at least.

Now all that's left to do
is bring this dish to your dear: a single taste

and what you wish for most, that most
dangerous of wishes, will certainly come true.

The hare sleeps with its eyes open

Not so much the all-seeing eye, the third eye, or the inner
eye, as the fabled 'eyes of night'

set up for dark work and focused on all manner
of goings-on, mostly by moonlight or torchlight,

the fiery cross, the backlit banner,
the mob at the telegraph office, the mob on the street,

the silent car with its brights
damped down, the sudden descent at dusk, the firefight

that looked, they said, just like electric sleet,
the turkey shoot, the burning collar,

the simple, intimate black and white
of the naked bulb in the windowless cellar.

~

And you yourself with that particle of deceit
though it's small enough to cheat the eye, and light as a
    feather.

The hare pounds the herb of immortality
in the moon

Something like pabulum, they said, and bitter,
which might speak of aloes. Of course, you can add
whisky and honey in equal measure

though maybe it's better
to choke it down as it comes, get used to that bad
taste if the upshot is you live for ever.

'A green winter makes for a fat churchyard.' Well, no
  more
of that to the hare's spoon-fed elect, no more
of the 'long barrow', the 'last goodbye', the 'debt to
  nature'.

And even less of the sad succession of wives
stepping off into darkness, of the habit most things have
of worsening day to day, of the slow but certain
  narcosis in rapture.

Plastic representations of the hare

The face of a silver coin, where two eagles, one white,
    one black, devour
a 'richly pregnant' hare. From this, Agamemnon could
    savour
the blood and ash of Troy, as a dog might sniff the air.

~

The emperor, Ming Ti, took to his grave the bare
necessities of death: rice, a kettle, chopsticks and bowl,
    a quire
of mitsumata, his brushes, his ink blocks, a small jade
    hare.

~

That Taiwanese with the fuzzy scut, won at the Easter
    fair,
give her pride of place on your chiffonier
close by the window: she'll stare down the moon from
    there.

The hare-headed goddess

A natural redhead as anyone here can tell
from the porno-star Swan Vestas pubic strip, a soft
tuft of the same in the small of her back. It's a gift,
the way she does what she does, up on a pedestal

showing those oh so edible parts
to the drifters, the reps, the long-haul truckers,
the usual assortment of arseholes and motherfuckers
with their deep and abiding love of the liberal arts

as exemplified by the way she shakes her stuff,
the way she rides that boa, the way
she dry-humps the bar, all pay-and-play:
that's pay till it hurts, my friend, and play it rough.

Were you thinking of going round to ask for a date?
Don't waste your time: she's already slipped out the back
leaving her tits and arse on the rack
along with her loppy ears, her bobtail, her old fur coat.

The hare sign signifies leaping

By *leaping* is meant *rising* which hints at *dawn* and *east*.
From *rising* we get *tumescence*, bringing us straight to
  man and *beast*.

The hare used as a hieroglyph for the auxiliary verb 'to be'

With the dogs that close, her only hope
was to make a dash
for a nearby thicket of text, where she elbowed into a gap
somewhere between *arrish*
and *art*, then turned arsy-versy to send her scent upwind.

'I'm not myself, as you see. I wish
I could tell you more, but the fact is you won't get a blind
word out of me after this, or see me much; I shall slip
back and forth between *dark* and *dawn*,
between *gift* and *graft*, between *scholar* and *scorn*,

being always the one and only, the turncoat, the
    mouthpiece, John Doe,
being all things to all comers, being just so.'